Bilingual Edition

Let's Draw with Shapes™

Edición bilingüe

Let's Draw a Bird with Shapes

Vamos a dibujar un ave usando figuras

Joanne Randolph

Illustrations by Emily Muschinske

Traducción al español:
Mauricio Velázquez de León

The Rosen Publishing Group's
PowerStart Press™ & **Editorial Buenas Letras**™
New York

Published in 2005 by The Rosen Publishing Group, Inc.
29 East 21st Street, New York, NY 10010

First Edition

Book Design: Emily Muschinske

Photo Credits: p. 23 © W. Perry Conway/CORBIS.

Library of Congress Cataloging-in-Publication Data

Randolph, Joanne.
Let's draw a bird with shapes = Vamos a dibujar un ave usando figuras / Joanne Randolph ; illustrations by Emily Muschinske ; translation by Mauricio Velázquez de León.
    p. cm. — (Let's draw with shapes = Vamos a dibujar usando figuras)
Includes index.
ISBN 1-4042-7555-X (library binding)
1. Birds in art—Juvenile literature. 2. Drawing—Technique—Juvenile literature.
3. Geometry in art—Juvenile literature. 4. Shapes—Juvenile literature. I. Title: Vamos a dibujar un ave usando figuras. II. Muschinske, Emily. III. Title. IV. Let's draw with shapes.

NC782.R35 2005b
743.6'8—dc22

2004006257

2

Due to the changing nature of Internet links, PowerStart Press has developed an online list of Web sites related to the subject of this book. This site is updated regularly. Please use this link to access the list:
http://www.buenasletraslinks.com/ldwsh/ave

Contents

Contenido

Draw a red circle for the body of your bird. Add a red oval for the head.

Dibuja un círculo rojo para hacer el cuerpo de tu ave. Agrega un óvalo rojo para hacer la cabeza.

5

Add an orange square to start the wing of your bird.

Dibuja un cuadrado anaranjado para comenzar a dibujar el ala de tu ave.

7

Draw a yellow square to start the other wing of your bird.

Dibuja un cuadrado amarillo para comenzar la segunda ala de tu ave.

9

Add two green triangles to the wing of your bird.

Agrega dos triángulos verdes al ala de tu ave.

Add two blue triangles to the other wing of your bird.

Agrega dos triángulos azules a la segunda ala de tu ave.

13

Add two purple triangles for the tail of your bird.

Agrega dos triángulos de color violeta para hacer la cola de tu ave.

Draw a pink half circle for the beak of your bird.

Dibuja un semicírculo rosa para hacer el pico de tu ave.

17

Add a small black circle for the eye of your bird.

Dibuja un pequeño círculo negro para hacer el ojo de tu ave.

Color in your bird.

Colorea tu ave.

A bird uses its wings to fly.

Las aves usan sus alas para volar.

Words to Know/Palabras que debes saber

beak/**pico**   body/**cuerpo**   head/**cabeza**   wing/**ala**

Colors/ Colores

 red/rojo

orange/anaranjado

yellow/amarillo

green/verde

blue/azul

purple/violeta

pink/rosa

black/negro

Shapes/ Figuras

circle/**círculo**   rectangle/**rectángulo**

square/**cuadrado**   oval/**óvalo**

triangle/**triángulo**   half circle/**semicírculo**